BY A. DUGAN AND THE EDITORS OF CONSUMER GUIDE

FITNESS OVER 40

FOR MEN ONLY

BEEKMAN HOUSE
New York

CONTENTS

THE FITNESS OVER 40 PROGRAM 3

Follow these guidelines to get the best results from the fitness program. Get ready to start looking and feeling younger and stronger.

THE EXERCISE ROUTINES

Start your training program with the Beginning Level 1 exercise routine, regardless of your present fitness level. You'll gradually work your way through to the Intermediate and Advanced routines as you build your strength and endurance.

Louis Weber, President
Publications International, Ltd.
3841 West Oakton Street
Skokie, Illinois 60076

Printed and bound by Pomurski tisk, Yugoslavia

10 9 8 7 6 5 4 3 2 1

Library of Congress Catalog Card Number: 84-61073

ISBN: 0-517-45255-3

Cover design: Jeff Hapner and Barbara Clemens
Book design: Jeff Hapner and Brenda Kaharl-Archambault
Photography: Sam Griffith Studios
Models: Niles McMaster, John Rusk, Chuck Swenson

The years over forty can and should be the best years of your life. You probably have more time to devote to yourself, to direct your energies toward your own interests and achieve the rewards of a productive life. The single most important requirement for living a full and active life is having the physical well-being to pursue your goals. Exercise is the key to attaining and maintaining physical fitness and well-being.

The Fitness over 40 Program is designed to raise your fitness level to its highest potential. Following the program will help you increase your strength, flexibility, coordination, balance, and endurance. Not only will you feel strong, healthy, and vitally alive, but you will also look better—and continue to look better—for the rest of your life.

Stop the Clock and Turn It Back

The old saying "you're as young as you feel" is true. Aging is to a great extent self-determined. It is not a slide everyone goes down at the same rate. Many travel more quickly than others—not because of what they do, but because of what they don't do to help slow down the aging process. You have a chronological age—your age in years. But you also have a physiological age—the age that reflects your actual physical condition. Often the chronological age and the physiological age are quite different. A man with a chronological age of forty may have a physiological age of twenty or thirty. On the other hand, a man of thirty may have a physiological age of sixty. Although growth proceeds at a predictable rate, physiological age does not. Scientific evidence shows that exercise is the single most effective way to lengthen and improve the quality of life. A vital exercise program can change a man's fitness level to that of a man ten to twenty years younger.

No matter what your level of fitness, you can improve it at any age with a regular exercise program. The heart can increase its capacity for work. The muscles can become more efficient in using oxygen from the blood, and thus can do more work without putting as great a demand on the heart. Muscle strength can be increased so that the muscles have more tone and endurance. Ligaments and joints can become more flexible, so that you can take part in sports with decreased risk of pain or injury. You can play golf, tennis, softball, or racketball without experiencing tennis elbow, lower back pain, or hamstring pulls. Aerobic conditioning can strengthen your heart and lungs, to give you greater endurance to keep going without undue fatigue. Our bodies were designed to be active at all stages in life. The unexercised body is not working at its full potential. The years from forty to sixty are the ones in which you must work to achieve this potential without physiologically aging. Stay with this fitness program, and the rewards will be great. Not only can you look ten or more years younger, but you'll feel younger physically and mentally as well. Remember, the gauge for determining your physiological age is performance. You can direct your body to achieve its maximum output—whether at work, at play, or under the stresses of daily living.

PROGRAM GUIDELINES

1 It is recommended that you consult your doctor before beginning this or any other exercise program.
2 If you have not been exercising regularly or if you have a medical history that would limit activity, consult your doctor as to which exercises in this program are best for you.
3 Wear comfortable clothing so that your movements are not restricted. Do not wear rubberized or plastic suits, which do not allow body heat to escape. Heat exhaustion can result from exercising in these suits.
4 Wear an athletic shoe or firm support shoe which will help absorb any shock that may occur to the ankles, knees, and back.
5 While exercising, breathe normally through the mouth and the nose. Do not hold your breath at any time.
6 Avoid dizziness by pausing briefly before changing direction.
7 Stop exercising if you feel dizzy or nauseated.
8 Start slowly, doing each exercise the recommended number of times or fewer. Then work up gradually to the advanced number of repetitions.
9 Do not overstress yourself. Work to the point of fatigue—not to the point of exhaustion or strain.
10 Do not rush through the program. Remember that speed is not as important as endurance.

11 Throughout the program, monitor your heart rate and watch for signs of undue strain or injury.

12 When doing the knee bends, avoid lowering the hips below the knees to prevent stress on the cartilage in the knees.

13 There is no one best time to exercise. Set aside a time during the day that is best for you. Try to do the program at the same time each day you work out, so that it becomes a vital part of your normal routine.

14 Eat only in moderation during the two hours before you exercise; otherwise nausea could occur.

Using the Fitness Program

This program follows the medically recommended principle of gradually increasing the workload placed on the body. Slowly building strength and flexibility is the most effective way to exercise, and it decreases the risk of strain and injury. In this program, the workload is gradually increased in two ways: by increasing the number of times you repeat each exercise, and by progressing to more difficult exercise routines.

The program is divided into Beginning, Intermediate, and Advanced sections. In each section, there are two complete exercise routines, Level 1 and Level 2. As you work your way up through these six exercise routines, the exercises gradually become more demanding on the body. The number of times you should repeat each exercise is indicated in the exercise instructions. When you first start a new level, do the number of repetitions indicated under "Start." Then as you get stronger, gradually add repetitions (adding one or two at a time) until you work up to the number of repetitions indicated under "Advance to."

No matter what your present level of fitness, it is recommended that you start with the Beginning Level 1 routine, and then gradually work your way up through to the Intermediate and Advanced levels. Perform the starting number of repetitions in the Beginning Level 1 routine three times a week, alternating exercise days with days of rest. As your body becomes adjusted to the exercise routine and it is easier for you to do, gradually increase the number of repetitions until you reach the advanced number of repetitions indicated. Depending on your own body and physical condition, this should take three to five weeks.

When you have reached the advanced repetitions and can do them easily, add one day from the Beginning Level 2 program, doing the starting number of repetitions, so that you are now working four days a week. Continue with this workout plan for two weeks, and then drop the Beginning Level 1 and continue with Beginning Level 2, doing the starting number of repetitions for four days a week. Follow this routine for three weeks, gradually increasing the number of repetitions until you reach the advanced repetitions.

As you feel your body becoming stronger, drop one day of the Beginning program and add one day of the Intermediate Level 1 exercise group, beginning with the starting repetitions. Now you are doing three days of Beginning Level 2 advanced repetitions and one day of Intermediate Level 1 starting repetitions. Again as you progress, drop the Beginning workout and do four days of the Intermediate Level 1 with the starting repetitions, gradually moving to the advanced repetitions indicated.

Continue in this manner, progressing slowly until you have reached the Advanced Level 2 routine. When you have mastered Advanced Level 2, continue to work at that level three to five days a week. You can continue at that level indefinitely to maintain the fitness level you have achieved.

If you are off the program for any length of time, go back and start at the Beginning Level 1, and again work up slowly to Advanced Level 2. Remember, it only takes 72 hours for the body to start losing its strength and endurance! So keep with it. Supplement this program with any physical activity you enjoy, such as sports or dancing. If you're already an active person, this program will help you become better equipped to meet the physical and mental challenges of your favorite sports and activities.

Prescription for Success: Follow the Program Exactly

Each routine includes several different types of exercises; each type is essential to a sound fitness program. Each exercise routine begins with a few warm up or aerobic exercises. Warm up exercises increase breathing, circulation, and body temperature to prepare the body for the increased demands exercise places on it. The warm up exercises are followed by stretching movements. Stretching conditions ligaments, tendons, and connective tissue, which helps the body move with ease and agility and helps prevent injury. After the warm up and stretching, there are exercises for conditioning specific areas of the body. The routine ends with cool down exercises, which let the body return gradually to the pre-exercise state. Whenever you work out, do all the exercises in the routine in exactly the order given, so that you have a safe and effective workout.

When you begin the program, your routine might take from 20 to 25 minutes. As you advance, you will be working from 35 to 45 minutes. Beyond 45 minutes, the body tends to experience an overload effect, reaching a point of fatigue in which injury and unnecessary strain can occur. You should feel greatly exhilarated after the workout with a tremendous feeling of well-being, body strength, and control. If some muscle soreness occurs the next day, that is normal. Soreness will disappear as the muscles become ac-

customed to the new strain being placed on them. You are demanding more of your body now. And the more you demand, the more success you will achieve. Keep checking yourself in the mirror. Notice the difference in your muscle tone, breathing, and mental attitude. Just keep thinking, "I can look and feel ten years younger. I can turn back the clock!"

MONITORING YOUR BODY

To effectively build physical fitness, exercise must be neither too easy nor too difficult. One of the major benefits of this program is its emphasis on the "training effect." This term refers to improved physical capacity developed by regular aerobic exercise, which increases the body's strength and efficiency. The heart grows stronger, the lungs increase their capacity, and resting pulse and blood pressure decline, as do levels of pulse and blood pressure needed for a given activity.

Each person's response to exercise is different. Therefore, it is important that you carefully monitor your body's responses during your workout.

Monitoring the Heart by Taking the Pulse

The pulse is the direct extension of the functioning heart. A normal pulse (heart rate) in adults ranges between 60 and 80 beats per minute. Regular exercise may lower the resting pulse rate. The rhythm of the pulse reflects the rhythm of the heartbeat—weak or strong, fast or slow, regular or irregular. Checking your pulse during exercise tells you how your body is responding to the exercise and tells you the conditioning you are receiving from the training program.

When you exercise, your heart should be beating at 70 to 85 percent of its maximum rate for your age group. This 70 to 85 percent of your maximum heart rate is called your "training range" or your "target heart rate zone." If your heart rate is below 70 percent during exercise, you're not sufficiently challenging your heart and circulatory system. If it is above 85 percent, you're challenging it too much, and you should pause briefly to rest until the heart rate returns to 70 to 85 percent of your maximum heart rate.

To find out if you're in the "training range," stop exercising and

take your pulse for ten seconds and compare with the chart in this section. Multiplying by six will give you the beats per minute. If your heart rate is within the recommended training range, continue exercising. If it is lower, continue exercising, work a little stronger, and then take the pulse again. The training heart rate should last for 15 to 30 minutes, depending upon the intensity of exercise. Therefore, take the pulse after the warm up and again 15 to 20 minutes later. (The exercise instructions remind you to check the pulse after the warm up.) Notice that the training heart rate will improve as you advance through the program. However, do not try to attain the training heart rate when you first start the program and do not try to work up to it too quickly. Be sure to take the resting heart rate before you start exercising and again ten minutes after finishing the workout. The pulse should return to normal (the approximate beginning resting heart rate) by that time.

The pulse is usually taken:
1 At the radial artery, which is in the wrist just below the base of the thumb.
2 At the carotid artery,

THE FITNESS OVER 40 PROGRAM

TRAINING HEART RATES*
to Determine the Conditioning Effects of Exercise

Age	Beats in 10 seconds		Beats in 1 minute	
	Minimum 70%	Maximum 85%	Minimum 70%	Maximum 85%
40	21	26	126	156
45	21	25	126	150
50	20	24	120	144
55	19	23	114	138
60	19	23	114	138
65	18	22	108	132
70	17	21	102	126
75	17	20	102	120
80	16	19	96	114

*These figures are averages for healthy individuals. For exact figures for yourself, ask your doctor. If your age falls between the ages shown in the chart, follow the averages for the age higher than your own age.

which is in the side of the neck underneath the jaw bone.

3 At the inside of the elbow, just above the skin crease.

To take your pulse at the radial artery, place your first two fingers on the inside of your wrist just below your thumb. Count the number of beats for 10 seconds and then multiply that number by six to determine your pulse rate (the number of beats per minute).

Note: Exercisers should compare the resting heart rate taken at the carotid artery with the resting heart rate taken at the radial artery. If the carotid rate (in the neck) is consistently lower than the radial rate (in the wrist) over many different trials, it would be wise to use the radial count (in the

wrist) to monitor target heart rates.

Respiration
The normal adult breathing count is approximately 15 to 17 breaths per minute. Exercise training increases the breathing capacity of the lungs. Increased lung capacity permits you to do more work with a lower expenditure of energy or oxygen consumption. Since you use less oxygen for a given task, you have a greater margin of reserve and can continue high levels of performance for a longer period of time without fatigue. To test your lung capacity and efficiency:
1 Take a deep breath. Try to hold your breath for 40 seconds. Then slowly let your breath out for 5 more seconds.
2 Exhale, letting all the air out of the lungs,

and measure the circumference of the chest (placing the measuring tape around the back and across the pectoral muscles in front). Then inhale as deeply as possible, hold the breath, and measure again. There should be a difference (increase) of 2½ to 3 inches. Cigarette smoking, asthma, or bronchial problems will alter this number.

About every two weeks, check this difference in the measurements taken after exhaling and then after inhaling. As you work through the program, you should see a very gradual increase in your lung capacity. (Do not practice holding the breath and do not take continuous deep breaths, since these activities may lead to hyperventilation or dizziness.)

ENDURANCE

Endurance provides the basis for a zestful life. Exercises that build endurance help improve the functions of the entire body. Endurance is dependent upon heart and lung efficiency, which in turn influences the performance of other parts of the body.

In this fitness program, the endurance exercises are the aerobic warm ups (such as the run in place, race walk, run and kick, jumping, and hopping). Race walking is usually done moving forward; however, it can also be done in place as in this program. Contrary to a regular walk in place, race walking in place is done briskly, with the movement from the hips. The weight on the foot moves from the heel to the big toe. The supporting knee locks so that you get a massaging action in the legs. The muscles exert pressure on the veins as you move, thus improving the flow of blood back to the heart. The arms are swung across the body for greater heart conditioning. Notice that race walking is done early in the program because it provides good aerobic conditioning without too much effort or strain. However, as you advance in the program and become stronger (if you do not engage in any other physical activities or sports), you may want to follow a race walk, jog, run schedule on one of the days you are not following the exercise program—perhaps on the weekend.

Here is a walk, race walk, jog, run program for determined distances in suggested periods of time. To begin, start with a mile walk for several weeks, gradually increasing your pace until you feel you are ready to advance to combining walking with race walking. Then move to combining walking, race walking, and jogging. Then you might move to a combination race walk, jog, and run. Alternate among these different activities, doing whatever feels comfortable to you. Don't push yourself too hard. When you start to feel tired from race walking, for example, slow down to a walk. Don't push yourself to jog or run when you don't feel strong enough. Walking and race walking are also effective conditioning activities. If you have been walking or running and your time exceeds those shown in the chart, stay with your own walking or running program.

Week	Distance	Time
1	1 mile	20 min.
2	1½ miles	30 min.
3	2 miles	40 min.
4	2 miles	40 min.
5	2½ miles	50 min.
6	3 miles	60 min.

Three miles is the suggested maximum run. As you become stronger, your time for this run should decrease; however, remember that endurance is much more important than speed.

After your walking, race walking, jogging, or running, it is very important to do some stretching exercises. The Training Stretch, the Pike Stretch, and the Relaxer exercises (included in the Advanced Level 2 routine of this fitness program) are especially good stretches to do after walking or running.

FUELING FOR ENERGY

From birth and continuing throughout life, the nutritional needs of the body are constantly changing. Age, heredity, stress, disease—all play a part in the wearing away and breaking down of body functions. Diet is one of the most important factors in the constant growth and repair of the body that continues through-

out life. While a good diet can't guarantee that you will be in good health, you can't be in good health *unless* you live on a good diet.

After the age of thirty, the basal metabolism decreases slightly from year to year. This means that there is a slowdown in the metabolic rate (the rate at which we use energy and burn calories). Along with this slowdown, we tend to be less active and engage in less strenuous activities, sports, and exercise. This means that we are burning fewer calories in our daily routine. It also means that we need fewer calories to maintain necessary body functions. The recommended daily calorie allowance for men at age twenty-five is 3,200 calories a day. At age forty and up, it is 2,400 calories per day. This means that we must pay attention to calorie intake and become more active. Food habits do not always follow our food needs. But by analyzing your nutritional needs, you can watch what you are eating so that you can continue to maintain a healthy body.

Your nutritional goals should be:
• To meet your daily needs for protein, carbohydrates, fat, vitamins, and minerals.
• To control calories and maintain a desirable weight.
• To avoid eating excessive amounts of food containing saturated fat and cholesterol.
• Watch the 3 S's—sugar, starch, and salt.
• The key word is *moderation* in everything—especially your diet.

EXERCISE!

"If exercise could be packed into a pill, it would be the single most widely prescribed, and beneficial, medicine in the Nation," says Robert N. Butler, M.D., Director of the National Institute on Aging. Each year, more and more scientific evidence points to the truth of this statement. Regular physical activity can help the human body repair itself to an amazing degree. When combined with good eating habits, exercise can help you lose weight or maintain your ideal weight, give you more energy, help you sleep better and feel less tense, improve your appearance and self-confidence, and contribute to good mental health by keeping you active.

Start now and keep it up!

A Stand with the knees slightly bent, arms at waist height, hands in fists.

B Swing forward to rise up on the toes, then back down onto the heels. At the same time, swing both arms forward and back.

Start: 25 times
Advance to: 50 times

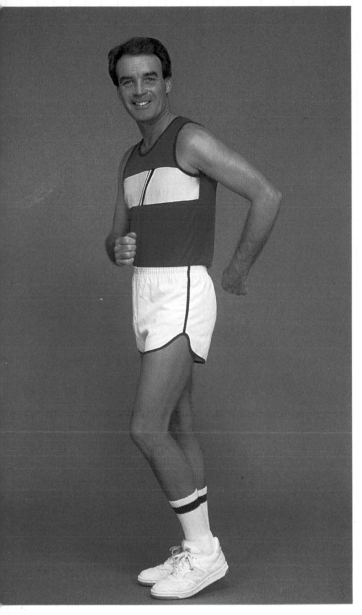

A Stand with the weight on the right foot, left knee slightly bent. Bend one arm in front of the chest, one arm in back, with the hands in fists.

B Race walk in place. Lift the left heel high. Then change foot positions, lifting the right heel and lowering the left heel. Move at a fast pace, alternating left and right feet, swinging arms forward and back at the same time.

Start: 100 counts
Advance to: 150 counts

Check pulse.

Always keep the arms bent at a 90-degree angle. Pump the arms vigorously. You should be puffing slightly after this. Good. That means you are conditioning the heart and lungs.

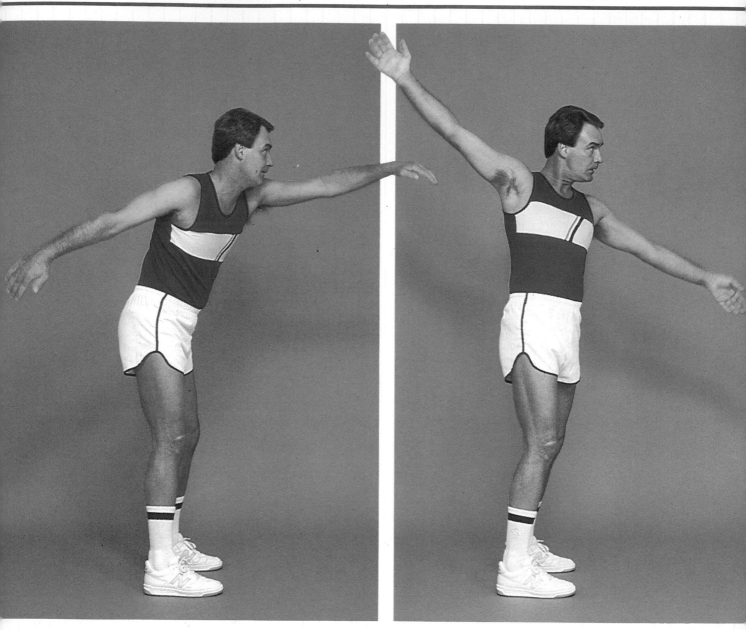

A Stand with the feet apart, knees slightly bent. Circle the arms forward, alternating right and left arms.

Start: 15 times
Advance to: 25 times

B Continuing the action, circle the arms backward, alternating left and right arms.

Start: 15 times
Advance to: 25 times

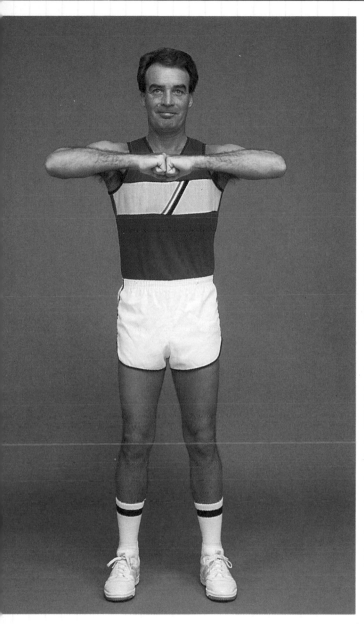

A Stand, elbows bent at chest height, hands in fists, knuckles pressed together.

B Keeping the elbows up, slowly press both arms back as far as possible. Hold for 2 counts. Return to starting position and repeat.

Start: 10 times
Advance to: 25 times

REACH FOR IT

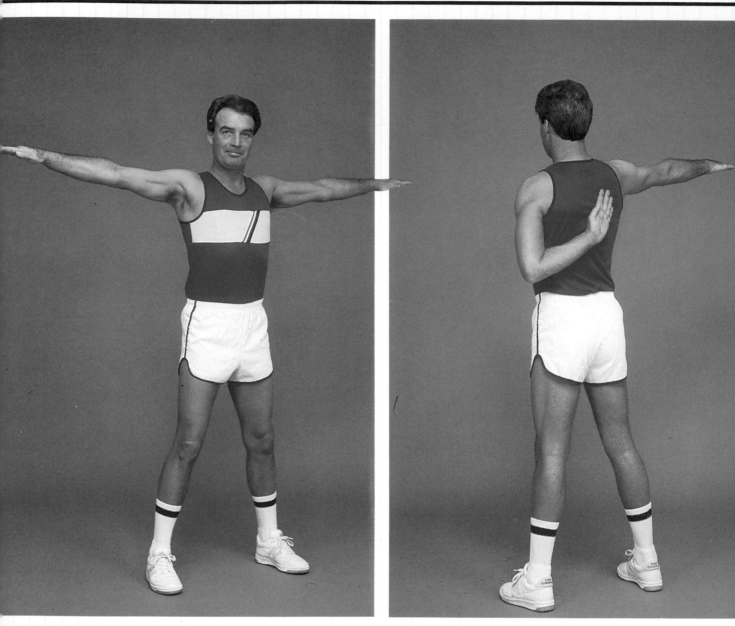

A Stand with the feet wide apart, knees slightly bent, arms extended to the sides at shoulder height.

B Bend the left arm to place the hand behind the back, reaching up as high as possible. Return. Repeat with the right arm, alternating left and right.

Start: 15 times
Advance to: 30 times

This exercise helps maintain flexibility in the arms and shoulders.

A Stand with the weight on the right leg, left leg to the side with the weight on the toes, arms extended directly out to the sides.

B Pull the left knee up toward the chest, encircling the knee with both arms. Return leg to floor. Repeat with the right leg.

Start: 10 times left, 10 times right
Advance to: 15 times left, 15 times right

Great for the waistline, lower back, and hips.

LUNGE

A Stand with the arms overhead, weight on left leg, right leg bent so that the lower leg is crossed up in back.

B Lunge to the side with the right leg, at the same time extending the arms out to the sides. Return to starting position. Repeat on left side.

Start: 10 times right, 10 times left
Advance to: 15 times right, 15 times left

Excellent for strength and flexibility in the legs and arms.

A Sit on the floor with the knees bent, feet flat on the floor, hands clasped behind the neck.

B Slowly uncurl the back down to the floor.

C Release the hands from behind the neck, and clasp one knee to the chest. Holding the knee, return to the sitting position.

Start: 10 times
Advance to: 25 times

This exercise strengthens the back and stomach.

A Sit on the floor with the legs wide apart, toes up, arms extended straight out from the shoulders, torso erect.

B Twist to the left and try to touch the right hand to the left foot, reaching as far as possible. Return to starting position. Then twist to the right. Continue, alternating left and right.

Start: 10 times
Advance to: 25 times

Stretch those hamstring muscles at the back of the thighs.

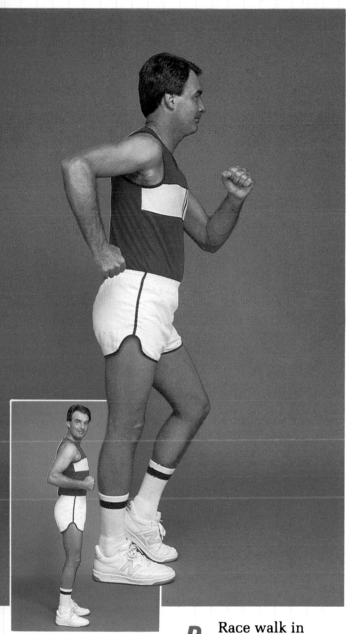

A Stand with the knees slightly bent, arms bent at waist height.

B Race walk in place, alternately lifting heels and swinging arms forward and back.

C Now run in place.

Start: Race walk for 25 counts, then run for 25 counts. Do 3 times for a total of 150 counts.

Advance to: Race walk for 50 counts, then run for 50 counts. Do twice for a total of 200 counts.

A Stand with the weight on the left leg, right leg to the side with the weight on the toes, arms at waist height.

B Hop twice on the left foot, then twice on the right foot. Do this in a continuous motion, swinging from one foot to the other, moving the arms forward and back at the waist in an easy swing. You should feel hot and start breathing more rapidly and deeply as you condition the heart and lungs.

Start: 50 counts
Advance to: 100 counts

Check pulse.

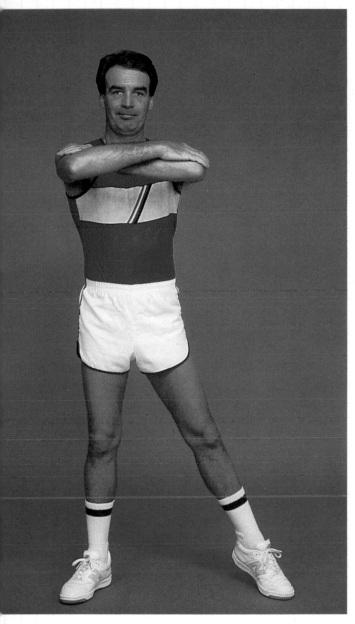

A Stand with the weight on the right leg, left leg to the side with the weight on the toes. Fold the arms in front of the chest.

B Press the arms to the left. At the same time, raise the left leg up to the side as high as possible. Return to starting position.

Start: 10 times on each side
Advance to: 15 times on each side

A Stand with the feet slightly apart, arms extended out to the sides from the shoulders.

B Lunge to the side with the left leg, bending the left knee. Bend the torso, and touch both hands behind the knee. Return to starting position. Repeat to the right.

Start: 10 times left, 10 times right
Advance to: 15 times left, 15 times right

This is a complete body exercise.

A Stand with the feet wide apart, left hand on the hip, right arm in an arc overhead, knees locked.

B Bend to the left side from the waist, pressing the right arm to the left. Return to starting position. Repeat on each side.

Start: 10 times left, 10 times right
Advance to: 15 times left, 15 times right

KNEE BEND

A Stand with the weight on the toes, feet wide apart, back straight, hands on hips.

B Bend the knees until the thighs are parallel to the floor. Return to starting position.

Start: 10 times
Advance to: 15 times

This exercise is excellent for building strength and flexibility in the legs and back. If you wish, do the exercise holding onto a chair.

Caution: To avoid stress on the knees, do not let the hips go lower than the knees.

A Start in a hurdler's sit, with the right knee bent back, left leg extended to the left side, arms out to the sides from the shoulders, torso erect.

B Twisting to the left, reach for the left foot with the right hand. Return to starting position. Repeat on each side.

Start: 10 times left, 10 times right
Advance to: 15 times left, 15 times right

Do this slowly to tighten the waistline and stretch the quadriceps in the front of the thighs.

SWING IT

A Sit on the floor with the legs wide apart, arms extended out to the sides from the shoulders, torso erect.

B Raise the right leg, and swing it across toward the left to touch the right leg with the left hand. Return to starting position. Repeat with each leg.

Start: 5 times right, 5 times left
Advance to: 10 times right, 10 times left

For the waistline, back, and hamstring muscles in the back of the thighs.

A Lie on the floor, hands clasped behind the head, knees bent, feet flat on the floor with the feet and knees slightly apart.

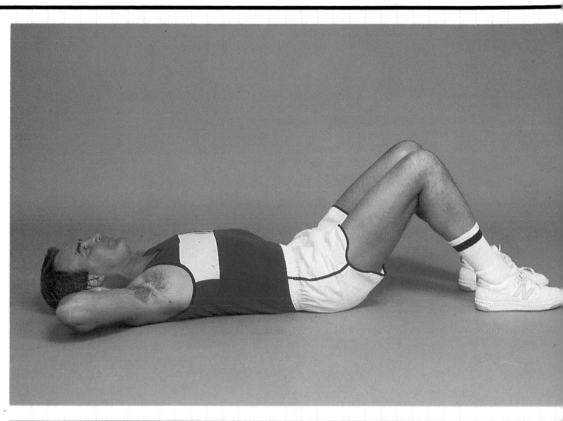

B Curl the head and shoulders up off the floor. At the same time, press the lower back into the floor. Return to starting position.

Start: 10 times
Advance to: 20 times

SCISSORS

A Lie on the back, hands clasped behind the head. The head may be up off the floor or resting on the floor—whichever feels better for the back. Extend both legs straight up.

B Swing the legs forward and back, alternating left and right legs.

Start: 10 counts
Advance to: 20 counts

Good for the back and the stomach muscles, as well as for blood circulation in the legs.

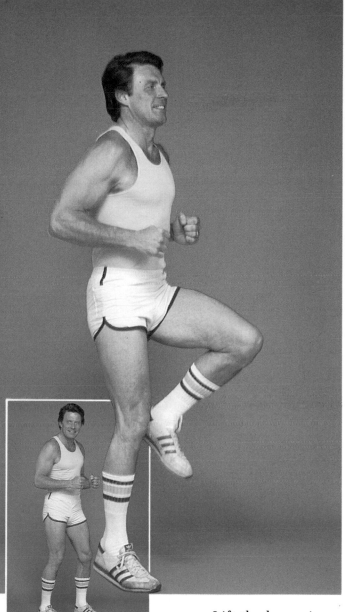

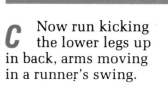

A Stand with the knees slightly bent, arms at waist height, hands in fists.

B Lift the knees in an easy run in place.

C Now run kicking the lower legs up in back, arms moving in a runner's swing.

Start: Run for 25 counts, kick for 25 counts.

Advance to: Run for 50 counts, kick for 50 counts. Do twice, for a total of 200 counts.

EASY JUMP AND HOP

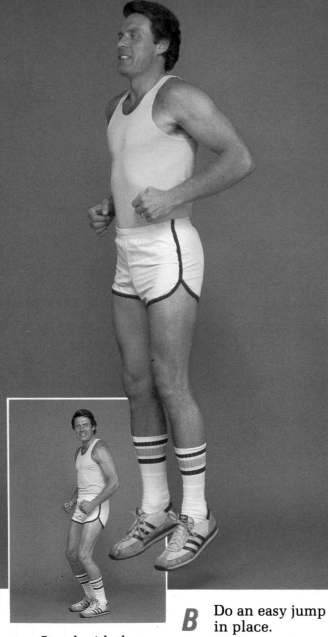

B Do an easy jump in place.

A Stand with the knees slightly bent, arms at waist height, hands in fists.

C Hop on the right foot, then on the left.

Start: Jump 10 times, hop on the right foot 10 times, and hop on the left foot 10 times. Do 3 times, for a total of 90 counts.

Advance to: Repeat as above 5 times, for a total of 150 counts.

Check pulse.

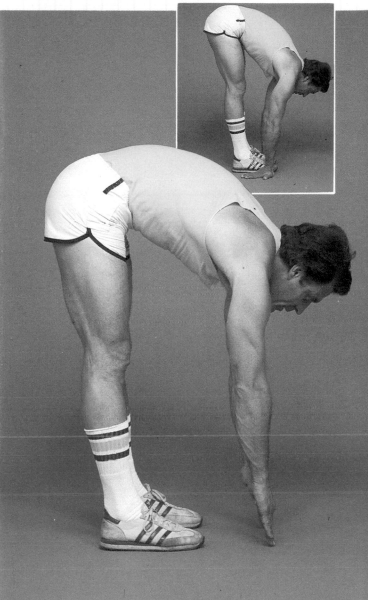

A Stand with the feet together, torso bent, fingertips on the floor in front of the toes.

B Very slowly try to straighten the legs. Return to starting position.

Start: 5 times
Advance to: 5 times, but place hands outside of feet with the fingers turned back toward the heels.

Stretch the hamstring muscles in the back of the thighs to keep them comfortably flexible and strong.

A Stand with right knee bent, right hand holding right ankle, left leg straight, left arm hanging so that the hand is touching the floor.

B Holding the ankle, slowly straighten the right leg back as far as possible. At the same time, press the left arm up overhead, and turn the head and torso to look at the left arm. Hold for 5 counts. Return to starting position. Repeat on each side.

Start: 5 times left, 5 times right
Advance to: Same

Do very slowly for a complete stretch.

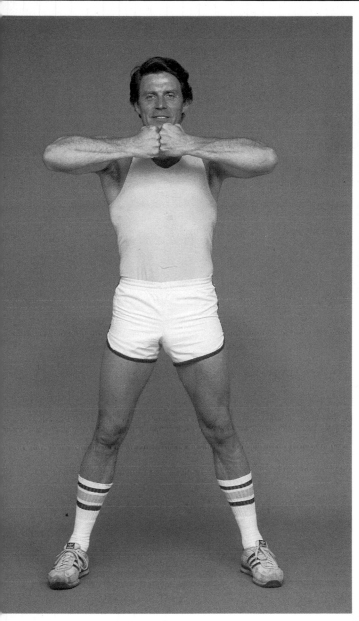

A Stand with the feet wide apart, arms bent with the hands in fists, knuckles pressed together in front of the chest.

B Maintaining the arm position, twist to the left, pressing the arms to the left as far as possible. At the same time, turn the head to the left to look at the far elbow. Return to starting position. Repeat on both sides. Do not alternate right and left.

Start: 5 times left, 5 times right
Advance to: 10 times left, 10 times right

31

CONTRACT THOSE MUSCLES

A Stand with the feet wide apart, right hand behind the neck, left hand on the left thigh.

B Bend the left knee and touch the right elbow to the left knee. Keep the hand on the thigh to support the back. Return to starting position. Repeat to right side.

Start: 5 times left, 5 times right
Advance to: 15 times left, 15 times right

Feel the muscle contraction in the stomach and legs.

A Stand in a 3-point stance, with the feet wide apart, knees bent so that the thighs are nearly parallel to the floor, left hand on left thigh to support the back, right knuckles on the floor.

B Keeping the hands in place, slowly lift the hips, straightening the knees as far as possible. Return to starting position.

Start: 10 times
Advance to: 15 to 20 times

This exercise strengthens and stretches the hamstring muscles in the back of the thighs.

SIT-UP

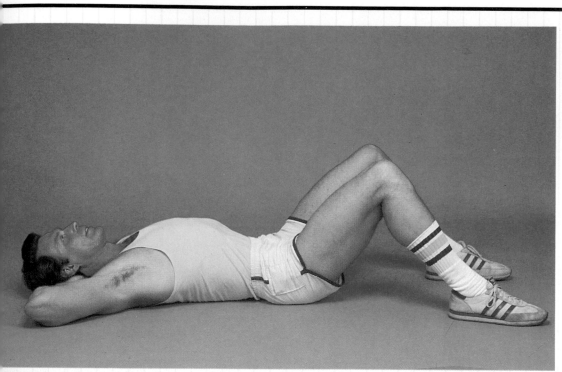

A Lie on the floor, hands clasped behind the head, knees bent, feet flat on the floor.

B Sit up and touch the left elbow to the right knee. Return to starting position. Repeat, touching right elbow to left knee. Continue, alternating right and left.

Start: 10 times
Advance to: 15 to 20 times

Flatten that stomach and strengthen the back.

Do this exercise sitting on a mat, a thick carpet, or a folded towel.

A Lie on the back, hands clasped behind the neck. The head may be up off the floor or resting on the floor—whichever feels better for the back. Extend both legs straight up with the feet flat.

B Slowly lower both legs to the floor, pressing the back into the floor.

C Then bend the knees into the chest. Return the legs straight up and repeat.

Start: 5 times
Advance to: 10 times

Do this exercise lying on a mat, a thick carpet, or a folded towel.

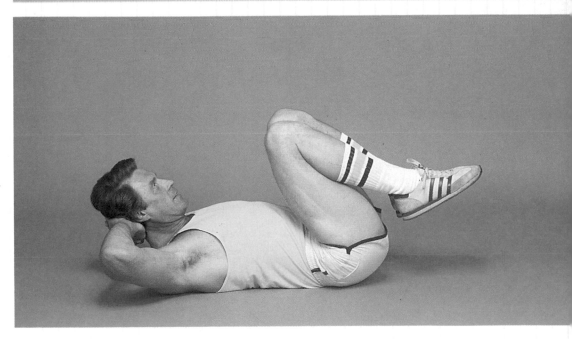

A Lift the knees in an easy run in place.

B Then run kicking forward. Move the arms in a runner's swing.

Start: Run 50 counts, kick 50 counts. Do twice for a total of 200 counts.

Advance to: Run 50 counts, kick 50 counts. Do 3 times for a total of 300 counts.

A Stand with the weight on the right foot, left leg to the side with the weight on the toes, hands on the hips.

B Hop on the right foot, crossing the left leg up in back of the right leg. Then hop left, crossing the right leg up in back. Repeat, alternating right and left.

Start: 25 counts
Advance to: 50 counts

Check pulse.

GOOD TURNOUT

A Stand with the feet wide apart, hands clasped in front of chest, elbows out to the sides.

B Turn the palms out. Straighten the arms and press them to the right, leaning to the right with the press.

C Return to starting position. Then press straight forward. Return and press to the left. Repeat, pressing each time to the right, forward, and left.

Start: 10 times
Advance to: 15 times

A With the feet apart, bend the knees until the thighs are parallel to the floor. Lean forward and swing the arms forward.

B Keeping the chest parallel to the floor, straighten the legs and throw the arms straight back. Return to starting position.

Start: 10 times
Advance to: 15 times

A Stand with the feet slightly apart, arms at sides.

B Bend the left knee, and extend the right leg up to the side. At the same time, raise both arms out to the sides and touch the right foot with the right hand. Return to starting position. Repeat on both sides.

Start: 10 times right, 10 times left
Advance to: 15 times right, 15 times left

40

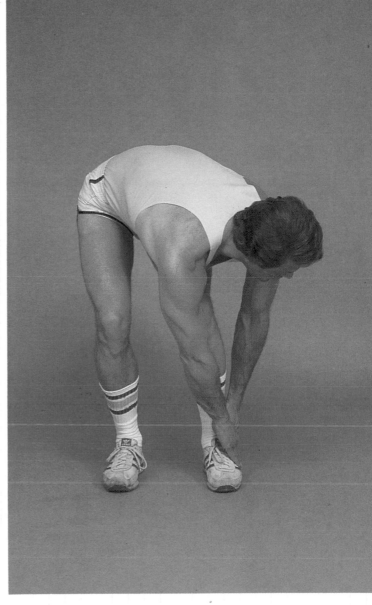

A Stand with the feet slightly apart, arms up overhead.

B Turn to the left, bend the knees, and touch the left ankle with both hands. Return to starting position. Then bend to the right touching the right ankle. Repeat, alternating left and right.

Start: 10 times
Advance to: 15 times

HURDLER'S LIFT

A Sit on the floor in a hurdler's position with the right knee bent back, left leg extended to the side, hands on the floor supporting the torso. Turn the left foot out to the side, with the outside of the foot resting on the floor.

B Raise the left leg up as high as possible, keeping it in the side position. Hold. Lower to starting position.

Start: 10 times left, 10 times right
Advance to: 15 times left, 15 times right

This exercise tightens the stomach and strengthens the inner thigh and groin area.

A Sit in a hurdler's position with the right knee bent back, left leg extended to the side. Lean on the left elbow, with the right hand holding the right ankle.

B Slowly raise the right leg and pull the ankle back as far as possible. Hold 5 counts. Return leg to floor and relax.

Start: 3 times each leg
Advance to: 3 times each leg, except hold the stretch for 8 counts

This exercise stretches the quadriceps in the front of the thighs and stretches the ligaments in the groin area.

ZAP THE "LOVE HANDLES"

A Sit on the floor, knees bent, feet off the floor, hands on the floor for support.

B Extend both legs to the right side, keeping the feet off the floor. Then bend the knees in to the starting position and extend the legs to the left side. Bend knees in to starting position and continue, alternating right and left.

Start: 10 times
Advance to: 15 times

Whittle that waistline!

Do this exercise sitting on a mat, a thick carpet, or a folded towel.

A Lie on the back with the right leg forward on the floor, left leg extended up, arms out to the sides, head resting on the floor.

B Keeping the arms and shoulders in place as much as possible, cross the left leg over to the floor on the right side. Touch as close as possible to the right hand. Return to starting position. Repeat. Then continue, crossing the right leg over to the left.

Start: 5 times left, 5 times right
Advance to: 10 times left, 10 times right

This exercise strengthens the stomach, back, and legs.

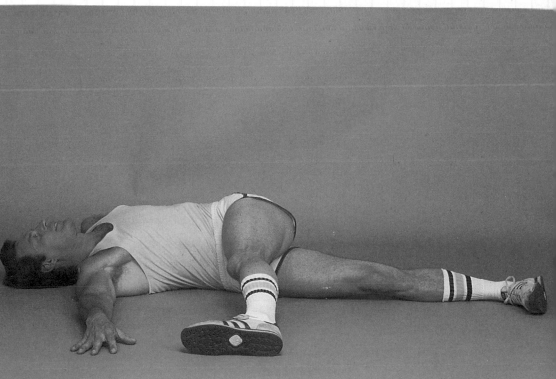

A Stand with the knees slightly bent, arms bent as if holding a jump rope.

B Lift feet, alternating right and left, following a boxer's run or jump. At the same time, turn the forearms and wrists as if jumping rope.

Start: 100 counts
Advance to: 150 to 200 counts

C Now do jumping jacks.

Start: 50 times, raising the arms just to waist height
Advance to: 50 times, raising arms overhead

Check pulse.

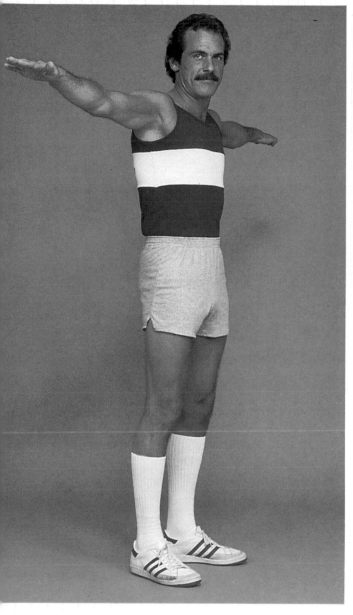

A Stand with the knees slightly bent, arms extended out to the sides.

B Raise the left leg straight forward and up, and try to touch the left ankle with both hands. Return to starting position. Repeat on each side.

Start: 10 times left, 10 times right
Advance to: 15 times left, 15 times right

BIG STRETCH

A Stand with the feet wide apart, knees bent, hands on knees.

B Move the left hip and thigh to the left, straighten the right leg, raise the right toes, and reach the right hand down toward the right foot. Return to starting position. Repeat to the other side. Continue, alternating right and left.

Start: 10 times
Advance to: 15 to 20 times

A Kneel on the hands and knees.

B With the weight on the right hand and right knee, bend the left knee into the chest, encircling the knee with the left hand.

C Extend the left leg straight out in back and the left arm straight forward. Return to starting position. Repeat with right leg and right arm.

Start: 10 times left, 10 times right
Advance to: 15 times left, 15 times right

This exercise conditions the back, shoulders, and neck.

Do this exercise kneeling on a mat, a thick carpet, or a folded towel.

A Lie on the stomach, legs extended, elbows bent, hands on the floor.

B Slowly push up to the knees, straightening the arms and arching the back.

Start: 5 times, pushing up to the knees only.

Advance to: 5 to 10 times, doing a complete push-up, lifting the whole body with the weight on the hands and toes.

A Sit in a hurdler's position with the right knee bent back, left leg extended to the side, arms folded in front of the chest.

B Raise the left leg and touch the arms to the left knee. Return to starting position. Repeat with each leg.

Start: 10 times left, 10 times right
Advance to: 15 times left, 15 times right

THE WINDMILL

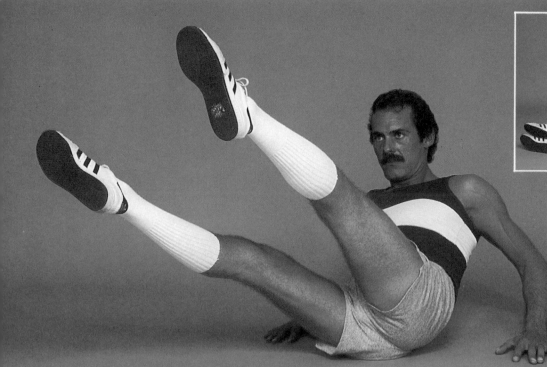

A Sit with both legs extended to the right side. Place the right elbow and the left hand on the floor for support.

B Raise the upper (left) leg, following with the right leg.

C Continue swinging both legs up and over to the left, in windmill fashion. Place the left elbow on the floor, and then lower both legs to the floor on the left side. Then swing the legs up and over again back to the right side.

Start: 10 times
Advance to: 20 times

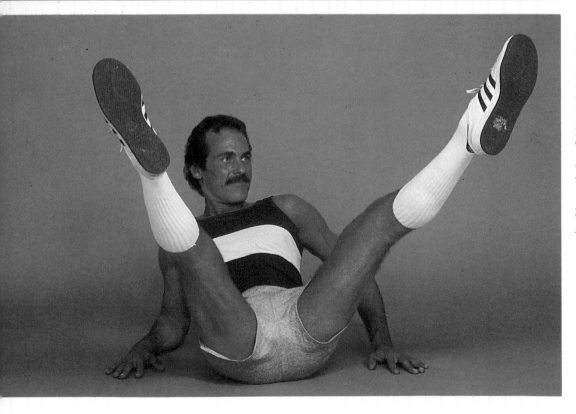

A Sit with both legs to the right side, weight on the right elbow, left hand behind the neck.

B Raise both legs and touch the left elbow to the knees. Lower legs to starting position. Repeat on both sides.

Start: 5 times right, 5 times left
Advance to: 10 times right, 10 times left

This is a good exercise for pulling in that waistline.

STRETCH STRESS RELIEF

A Lie on the back, arms out to the sides.

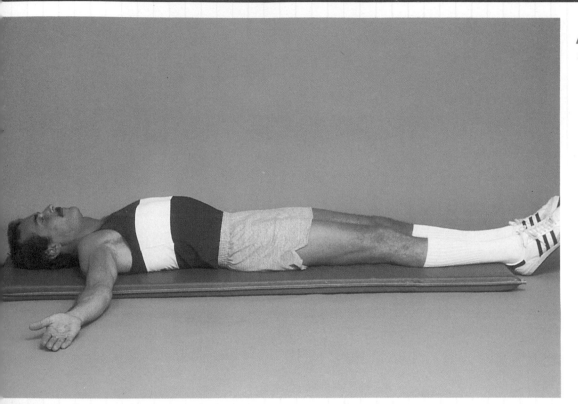

B Pull the right knee in toward the chest, grasping it with both hands. At the same time, lift the head and try to press the nose toward the knee. Hold for 5 counts. Return to starting position. Repeat with the left leg.

Start: 3 times each leg
Advance to: 5 times each leg

This exercise relieves tension and stress in the back.

If you wish, you may do this exercise in a standing position instead.

A Stand with the knees slightly bent, arms bent at the waist.

B Lift knees in an easy run in place, landing lightly on the balls of the feet and rolling from the outer arch of the foot to the heel. Swing the arms, pressing the elbows up in back.

Start: Run for 3 minutes.
Advance to: Run for 5 minutes.

Check pulse.

A Stand on the right leg with the left leg on a window sill or the back of a sturdy chair, arms at sides.

B Slowly bend forward, bending the right knee, and try to touch the left ankle. Hold for 5 counts. Repeat with other leg.

Start: Stretch once with each leg, bending the standing knee to reach.

Advance to: Stretch once with each leg, keeping the standing knee straight to reach.

This exercise stretches the lower back and the hamstring muscles and ligaments in the back of the thighs.

A Stand with the feet wide apart, left arm extended out to the side, right hand on thigh.

B Bend the right knee, keeping the right hand on the thigh to support the back. Bend the torso and place the left hand behind the right heel. Return to starting position. Repeat on both sides.

Start: 10 times right, 10 times left, with both feet flat on the floor
Advance to: 10 times right, 10 times left, raising the toe of the straight leg as you place the hand behind the heel

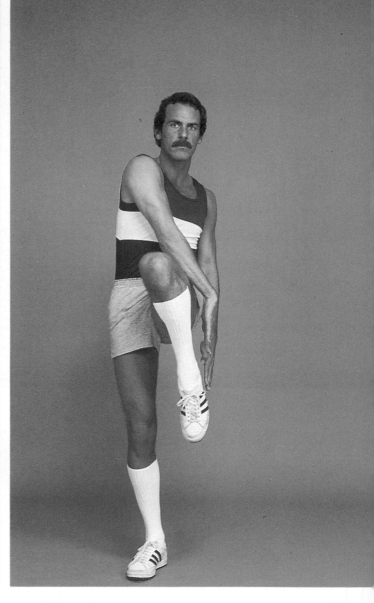

A Stand with the feet apart, hands extended straight up overhead.

B Raise the left knee and touch the outside of the left ankle with both hands. Return to starting position. Repeat on both sides.

Start: 10 times left, 10 times right
Advance to: 15 times left, 15 times right

A Stand with the knees bent so that the thighs are parallel to the floor, with the toes turned out slightly to the sides. Extend the arms out to the sides.

B Slowly lift both heels as high as possible. Lower heels to the floor.

Start: 10 times
Advance to: 15 times

A Sit on the floor with the knees bent, lower legs up and parallel to the floor, hands behind the head.

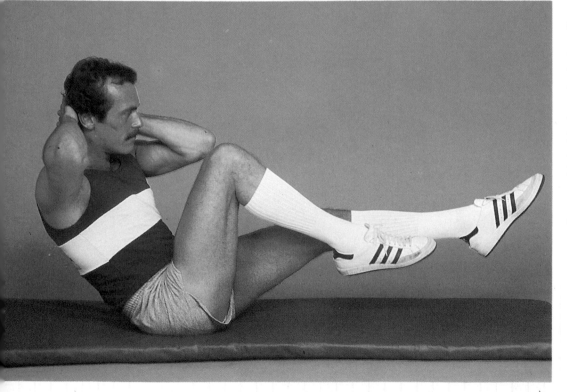

B Keeping both legs off the floor, pull the right knee in toward the chest and touch the left elbow to the right knee. Then pull the left knee in, touching it with the right elbow. Continue, alternating left and right.

Start: 10 times
Advance to: 15 times

A Lie on the back, hands clasped behind the head, knees bent into the chest. The head may be up off the floor or resting on the floor—whichever feels more comfortable for the back.

B Extend both legs straight up.

C Bend knees back in toward the chest. Then extend the legs forward. Continue, alternately extending legs up and then forward.

Start: 10 times
Advance to: 15 times

Extend the legs forward at an angle that is comfortable for the back— one that contracts the stomach muscles but does not stress the back.

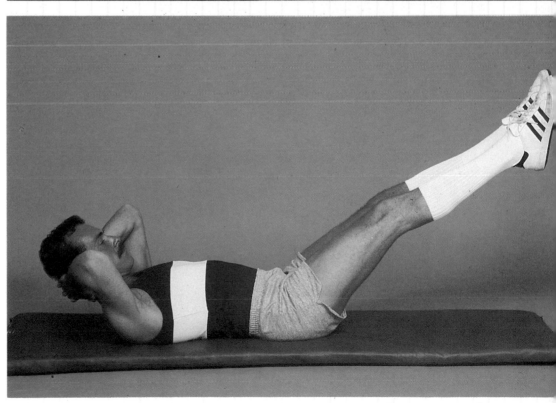

KICK OUT THE POT BELLY

A Lie on the back, hands under the head, knees bent into the chest. The head may be slightly up off the floor supported by the hands, or the head may be resting on the floor—whichever feels more comfortable for your back.

B Kick the legs up, alternating left and right.

C Then sit up and kick the legs forward, alternating left and right. Return to starting position.

Start: 10 kicks up, 10 kicks forward, for a total of 20 kicks

Advance to: 5 kicks up, 5 kicks forward. Do twice for a total of 20 kicks.

A Sit on the floor, legs extended forward with the knees slightly bent, hands behind the head.

B Keeping the knees bent, bend forward and try to touch the elbows to the knees. Hold for 5 counts.

Start: 3 times
Advance to: 6 times, holding for 10 counts

This is a good stretch for the lower back and the hamstring muscles in the back of the thighs.

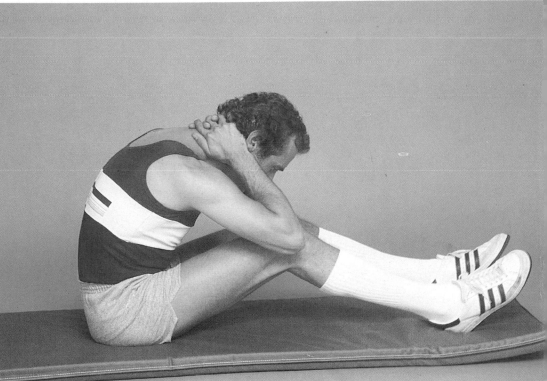

THE RELAXER

B Slowly uncurl the back, pressing the hips forward and gradually straightening the knees.

C Lift the torso to an upright position. Press the shoulders back, and reach up in a long stretch. Hold for 5 counts. Then relax.

Start: 3 times
Advance to: Same

A Stand with the feet apart, knees bent, arms hanging down, torso relaxed over the floor. Let the body hang loosely, like a rag doll.